Jean Andrews was born and grew up in the West of Ireland. A poet and translator of poetry, she teaches at the Department of Spanish, Portuguese and Latin American Studies at the University of Nottingham, UK.

Sí Orphans of the Plaintive Air

Poems and a Translation

by

Jean Andrews

Published 2013 by arima publishing

www.arimapublishing.com

ISBN 978 1 84549 585 5

© Jean Andrews 2013

All rights reserved

This book is copyright. Subject to statutory exception and to provisions of relevant collective licensing agreements, no part of this publication may be reproduced, stored in a retrieval system, or transmitted in any form or by any means, without the prior written permission of the author.

Printed and bound in the United Kingdom

This book is sold subject to the conditions that it shall not, by way of trade or otherwise, be lent, re-sold, hired out, or otherwise circulated without the publisher's prior consent in any form of binding or cover other than that which it is published and without a similar condition including this condition being imposed on the subsequent purchaser.

arima publishing
ASK House, Northgate Avenue
Bury St Edmunds, Suffolk IP32 6BB
t: (+44) 01284 700321

www.arimapublishing.com

Acknowledgements

I am grateful to Micheál Ó Conghaile at Cló Iar-Chonnachta, Co. Galway, Ireland, for permission to translate excerpts from Seán Ó Tuama's edition of the *Caoineadh Áirt Uí Laoghaire* (Lament for Arthur O'Leary).

Contents

Background Notes 5

Poems
  Deirdre 19
  Méabh 26
  Scáthach 29
  Gráinne 31
  Niamh of the Golden Hair 34
  Fionnuala 36
  Iseult 38
  Dearbhorgill 40
  Máire Rua 41
  Biddy Early 43
  The Fairy Tree at Latoon 45

Translation of the Lament for Arthur O'Leary 47
  I 48
  II 52
  III 54
  IV 57
  V 58

Rough Pronunciation Guide 61

Background Notes

Mythological Figures

The Ulster Cycle

The stories in this cycle may originate in 7th century lyrics and are preserved in Old and Middle Irish manuscripts from the 12th to the 15th centuries. The cycle centres on the adventures of the warriors of the Red Branch under the rule of Conchúr (Connor) Mac Neasa, king of Ulster, who held court at Eamhain Mhaca, today's Navan Fort, near Armagh.

Deirdre and the Sons of Usnach

The tale of Deirdre's elopement with Naoise and its tragic conclusion is one of the most enduring of the Ulster cycle. W.B. Yeats and J.M. Synge wrote plays on the topic. Before she was born, the druid Cathbhadh foretold that Deirdre would grow up to be very beautiful, that she would be fought over by warriors and kings and bring destruction on all around her. When Conchúr Mac Neasa heard this, he ordered that she be imprisoned until she reached womanhood, whereupon, in order to keep his realm safe and to profit from her beauty, he would take her to wife. Deirdre pre-empted this plan by inducing

Naoise Mac Uisnigh to abscond with her from under Conchúr's nose.

Méabh

Méabh (Maeve), queen of Connacht, was the most powerful foe of the kingdom of Ulster. She started a war against Ulster in order to capture the brown bull of Cooley, famed for its virility and power, so that she could trump her husband Ailill's boasts of the splendour of the white-horned bull in his herd. The white-horned bull had deserted Méabh's herd and moved to Ailill's because he considered it beneath him to be the chattel of a woman. Méabh's epic campaign led to single-combat between Ferdia, champion of Connacht and Cú Chulainn (the Hound of Culann, a *nom de guerre*, his given name was Setanta), champion of Ulster, who were friends from boyhood, and ultimately, to single-combat between the two bulls, with, in both cases, the Ulster champions emerging victorious.

Scáthach

Scáthach was a warrior of fearsome reputation to whom Cú Chulainn, renowned for his exploits as a boy with a *sliotar* (ball) and hurley, and Ferdia were sent as adolescents to learn the skills of fighting and chivalry. She is associated with the fort of Dún Scáith on the Isle of Skye. The base of the hurley, which is used to trap and hit the ball is called a *bos*.

The Fenian Cycle

These tales centre on Fionn Mac Cumhaill and his band of warriors, known as the Fianna. They served Cormac Mac Airt, high king of Ireland, whose court was based at Tara (Co. Meath). As with the Ulster Cycle, the origins of these tales may go back to the 7th century and they are found in manuscripts dating from the 8th century onwards.

Diarmuid and Gráinne

The elopement and pursuit of Diarmuid and Gráinne is similar to the tale of Deirdre and Naoise. The beautiful but wilful Gráinne was the daughter of the high king, Cormac Mac Airt. Betrothed by her father to his widowed warrior chieftain Fionn Mac Cumhaill, she was shocked to find that her intended bridegroom was older than her own father. Thereupon she decided, one way or another, to escape the fate in store for her. She tried to tempt various of the Fianna into running off with her, including Fionn's son Oisín, but they all refused, fearful of crossing Fionn. In the end, it was Diarmuid who succumbed to her stratagems, or who choose to be ensnared.

Niamh of the Golden Hair

This tale is one of the last in the Fenian cycle, and it brings the mythological Oisín into the time of St Patrick, in the 5th century. Niamh came across the sea to Ireland from the fabled Land of the Ever-Young, to the West, known as *Tír na n-Óg*. Her lover, however, was a mere mortal, although one of heroic proportions, and once he returned to Binn Éadair (Howth, Co. Dublin), the site of so many rousing Fianna adventures, and fell from Niamh's white horse onto the ground, he lost the conditional immortality conferred on him during his time in *Tír na n-Óg*. In the tale, Oisín became a Christian before he died of extreme old age.

The Mythological Cycle

This is a loose collection of tales recounting the deeds of the precursors of the Red Branch and the Fianna, such as the Tuatha Dé Danaan. They are believed to date back to the 7th century and, as with the other Gaelic cycles, are to be found in manuscripts dating from the 8th century onwards.

The Children of Lir

This tale forms a bridge between pagan and Christian Ireland, over the 900 years from when the children of Lear (Lir) were first cursed by their stepmother to when, as extremely old people, they emerged from the spellbound avian shapes in which they had lived for nearly a millennium to receive sanctuary, and eventual baptism, from nearby Christian monks.

The Arthurian Cycle

The tales in the Arthurian cycle were first recorded in twelfth century Norman literature and largely recount the chivalric feats of the knights of Camelot and their quest for the Holy Grail.

Tristan and Iseult

The story of the doomed love of Tristan and Iseult bears similarities to the fates of Deirdre and Naoise, and Diarmuid and Gráinne. The tale, in a variety of forms, emerged in France in the middle of the twelfth century and went on to become associated with the Arthurian Legends. Its prominence in Western culture perhaps culminates in Wagner's mid-19th-century music drama, *Tristan und Isolde*.

Broadly, Iseult, an Irish princess, was betrothed to the aged King Mark of Cornwall. Mark sent his foster son Tristan to fetch her. In some versions, Iseult, who had healing powers, cured Tristan of a mortal wound either on their voyage back to Cornwall or some time before they set sail. By accident or design, they ingested a love philtre on board ship and fell passionately in love. Unlike Deirdre and Gráinne, however, Iseult did not shirk her planned marriage to Mark, even though the lovers' loyalty to Mark and their engrossment in each other created an impossible tension which could only be resolved by their deaths.

Historical Figures

Dearbhorgill

Dearbhorgill (Dervorgill) was the wife of Tighearnán Mór Ua Ruairc, a Meath chieftain. She was abducted by the king of Leinster, Diarmuid Mac Murchadha (Dermot McMurrow) in 1152, probably as a hostage-taking manoeuvre which may have suited Dearbhorgill's own pragmatic ends as well. However, her husband, somewhat unusually, would not settle with Mac Murchadha and was eventually instrumental in the Leinster king's expulsion from Ireland in 1166. In 1169, the Normans invaded, partly abetted by Mac Murchadha who married his daughter Aoife to one of the foremost Norman warriors, Strongbow. Mac Murchadha's treachery became one of the most potent symbols of Irish loss of sovereignty, though it is likely the Normans would have attempted to encroach on Ireland with or without native encouragement.

On the commemoration plaque in the Nun's Church in Clonmacnoise, the inscription in Gaelic reads: 'the ill-fated Dearbhorgill who was kidnapped by Diarmaid Mac Murchú Caomhánach'. The inscription in English states that the church was finished in 1167 and Dearbhorgill lived there as a nun from 1170. The place is named in Irish as *Teampall na gCailleach*. The word *cailleach* means hag or wise woman and nun in the sense of anchorite or contemplative, thus 'the hag's church'.

Máire Rua

Máire Rua McMahon (1615/1616-1686) was the daughter of Mary O'Brien, whose own father was the O'Brien Earl of Thomond, and of Torlach Rua McMahon, lord of Clonderlaw in County Clare. She was called Máire Rua (Red Mary) for the colour of her hair, and to identify her as a member of her father, Torlach Rua's, branch of the McMahon clan. As a very young woman, she married Daniel Neylon of Dysert O'Dea, and had three sons by him: William, Daniel and Michael. After his death, she married Conor O'Brien of Leaghmenagh, in 1639, and they had four sons and four daughters: Donough, Teige, Turlough, Murrough, Honora, Mary and two other daughters who may have died of plague in 1651, the year of the Cromwellian Siege of Limerick.

Conor, a significant resistance leader, was mortally wounded in 1651 at the Pass of Inchicronan, at the hands of Cromwellian forces. He was taken back to his seat at Leaghmenagh Castle to die. It is said that General Ireton, then laying siege to the city of Limerick, had sent an assassin to dispatch him. Ireton himself died of fever in Limerick later on in the same year. After Conor's death, Máire Rua, realising that his act of rebellion would mean the forfeiture of all their lands, rushed to Limerick and offered to marry any of General Ireton's officers who would have her. This move appears to have forestalled confiscation of her lands and she married Cornet John Cooper two years later and gave him a son, Harry and possibly a daughter. Cooper grew wealthy through land and property speculation, lost some or all of it in more speculation, and predeceased her. A strategic decision was taken to bring up her eldest son by Conor, Donough, heir to the O'Brien lands, in the Anglican faith, to ensure his succession. He prospered and moved the family seat south to Dromoland. In 1686, co-incidentally the year of his mother's death, the baronetcy of Inchiquin was conferred upon him.

Various apocryphal legends grew up about Máire Rua before and after her death, most to do with colourful ways in which she might have disposed of her first and third husbands.

Biddy Early

Biddy Early (c.1798-1874) was a traditional herbalist and healer who became equally beloved and notorious in her own lifetime. She learned many of her cures from her mother, Ellen Early, whose surname she used. In her relatively long life, she had four husbands, all of whom died before her, and one son, Paddy, by her first husband, Pat Malley, from whom she became estranged when he reached adulthood.

She was famed for her cures throughout Co. Clare and neighbouring counties, and people travelled far and wide to consult her. She also treated sick animals. As was the way with folk healers, she did not charge her patients, leaving it up to them to offer what they could. Often, they paid in illicitly-distilled *poitín* or porter. The consequent prevalence of alcohol in her various abodes contributed to the opprobrium cast upon her, particularly by the Catholic Church which actively discouraged parishioners from going to see her with their ailments. However, this did not materially affect either her popularity or the reputed effectiveness of her cures, though it did lead to some very black legends growing up around her personality. In 1865, she faced an accusation of witchcraft at Ennis Courthouse though the case fell through due to lack of evidence.

Towards the end of her life, perhaps in knowing and sarcastic allusion to this ill-deserved reputation, she employed, as part of her practice, a mysterious bottle filled with a dark liquid into which she would gaze as she pondered the appropriate cure. She died in her mid-seventies, alone and in abject poverty.

Eibhlín Dhubh Ní Chonaill

Eibhlín Dhubh (Nelly, (c.1743- ?) was born into a well-to-do Co Kerry Catholic family, the O'Connells of Derrynane (Doire Fhíonaín). Derrynane would be come the seat of her nephew Daniel O'Connell (1775-1847), the towering Irish democratic political figure of the early nineteenth century. Derrynane House was built by Eibhlín's father, Domhnall Mór after his marriage to Máire Ní Duibh and was the first senioral dwelling to be constructed in Ireland since Cromwellian times. Máire produced twenty-two children and lived to the age of ninety or so, matriarch of her lands, family and discreet smuggling business to the end. Eibhlín was deemed flighty and self-willed by her mother and married off to an elderly member of the neighbouring Connor family when she was only fifteen, probably in 1758. Her spouse conveniently died six months later, with his teenage wife, none the more sober-minded, apparently cracking nuts for herself while the old man was on his deathbed. She was, all the same, sufficiently aware of her responsibilities to compose a lament for the deceased, a few odd lines of which still survive.

Some years later, in 1767, the widowed Eibhlín, while on a visit to her sister in Co. Cork, saw Art Ó Laoghaire riding down the street in Macroom. Her elder sister Máire had married James Baldwin of Macroom who, as Eibhlín attests in the poem, was not the most amenable of men. However, against all the expectations of the time, he had converted to Catholicism before the wedding, with the inevitable consequence that he spent much of the rest of his life worried about holding on to his estate. In complete contrast, Arthur O Leary was a carefree young blade and a dandy, a captain on leave (or he had resigned) from the Hungarian Hussars. Service in the armies of the European Catholic powers was the norm for well-born Catholics in an era when they were forbidden to join the British armed forces or indeed to carry arms. Eibhlín was smitten and a marriage was brought about on the 19th of December of that year, against the wishes of her family. They viewed Art, with reason, as an irresponsible hothead and womaniser with no understanding of the delicate line to be observed by Catholic landowners under the Penal Laws which discriminated, to varying degrees, against all non-Anglicans. He was nineteen, she was twenty-four and they went on to have six children, three of whom probably survived to adulthood. Art died at the age of twenty-six while Eibhlín lived to a comfortable, ripe old age. It is not known when or where she died. She is now regarded as a great poet and the last poet of the classical Gaelic tradition.

Just before his death, the long-standing animosity between Art and Abraham Morris, the High-Sheriff of Co. Cork, came to a head. For some time before this, Art had effectively been on the run from the sheriff's militia because of his refusal to sell a champion racehorse to him for £5.00. It was forbidden under the Penal Laws for a Catholic to own a horse worth more than that sum. Though this law was not often strictly observed, Abraham Morris sought to invoke it in order to humiliate Art O'Leary. On May 4th, 1773, having probably returned briefly to the family home, Art bade farewell to his wife and children and set out openly to kill Morris. Morris was made aware of Art's plan (Eibhlín names Seán Mac Uaithne as the informer) and took measures to protect himself, the upshot of which was Art's death at Carraig an Ime (Carriginima) later on that day, shot by one of the sheriff's soldiers.

His mare bolted and made her way back to the family home in Rath Laoich (Raghleagh). In her own account, Eibhlín heard her in the yard, dashed out, leapt on the horse and rode her back the seven miles of poor road to where her husband lay dead, in a pool of his own blood. As there was no priest to administer the last rites and none of the local people was willing to help, except for an old woman who covered the body with her cloak and knelt by the roadside to pray, Eibhlín symbolically cleansed her husband of the violence and disrespect he had suffered by drinking his blood there and then. She sang the first part of the lament that evening in a house in Carraig an Ime, probably that of the old woman who stayed by Art's corpse, and the second part of the *caoineadh* the next day at the funeral in Rath Laoich. Art's sister and father contributed verses to the lament, as was the tradition, but the bulk of it is of Eibhlín's invention.

The *caoineadh* survives in fragments preserved in traditional oral culture in Co. Cork and Co. Kerry. What is remarkable about Eibhlín's lament is that it has surivived at all and that so much of it transcends the genre to speak with a highly individual voice. This translation contains only those verses attributed to Eiblín in Seán Ó Tuama's edition of the *Lament for Arthur O'Leary, Caoineadh Airt Uí Laoghaire* (Baile Átha Cliath: An Clóchomhar Tta, 1961/6th reprint, 1979) and follows the numbering used in that edition.

The above remarks on the context of the poem are indebted to Ó Tuama's comprehensive introduction in the same edition. In the translation, I have tried, as far as possible, to render the literal meaning of the Gaelic original.

Present Day Issues

The Fairy Tree at Latoon

As a result of a campaign led by the writer and folklorist Eddie Lenihan in 1999, a multi-million pound EU-funded road system linking Shannon Airport to Ennis in Co. Clare had to be diverted, at considerable cost, from its original course so that a small hawthorn bush would not be disturbed. Lenihan argued that the hawthorn was a meeting-point for bands of pusillanimous, warring fairies (*sidhe* or *sí*, often 'shee' in English) from Munster on their way to do battle with enemy Connacht fairies and that any damage to the bush would result in serious otherworldly consequences. The bush stands close to an American-style motel which was popular with Irish Americans on nostalgic package tours in the sixties and seventies.

Pronunciation of Gaelic Names

I have decided to leave the Gaelic names in the original because there are very few cases where there is a universally used anglicisation and because Gaelic in Ireland has at least three dialects across which pronunciation varies a great deal. I have provided some very inelegant-looking approximations of my own pronunciation of these names at the end of this volume, for the curious and the persevering who have no acquaintance with the original language.

'Dun Sweeny adieu, for my love cannot stay,
And tarry I may not when love cries away'.

'Deirdra's Farewell to Alba',
Sir Samuel Ferguson,
Lays of the Western Gael.

Deirdre

The most beautiful woman in the world.
How often have we heard that one?

She saw the blood of a goat spilled on the snow
and a raven alight to take advantage.

That's what I want, said she:
'a man with blood on his cheeks, snow to cover his
 bones
and the feathers of a raven in his beard and hair'.

Her nurse looked askance.
She was locked away to await King Conchúr's
 pleasure,
when she came of age, in holy despite of his.

'There's one to meet your wish, *a chroí*', said she,
'at court right now, Naoise, son of the clan of
 Usnach'.

Who would come between a wilful wench
and the juices which run between her legs?

They met in secret, he had eyes to see and fell.
She decreed that they should run away to Scotland.
So they did, and for that, his loyal brothers, Ainle
    and Ardán,
who seemed to have no lives of their own in this,
and three hundred warriors, equally anonymous,
emigrated north-east to Alba so one pair of lovers
could enjoy each other's bodies in edgily-defended
    peace.

The king of Alba heard tell, after a while,
of this astonishing-looking woman,
squired by a herd of itinerant Ulstermen,
decided that his was the superior bed
and sent an army to detach her.

Many died, on both sides, none of the principals, of
    course.
They fled, instead, to an island in the sea, in-
    between.

Another period of relative ease?
Except that trouble had been predicted on her head
    at birth.
That was why Conchúr had her locked away
with only a tutor and a nurse,
and even why he vowed to take her to wife
when she was just an infant.
It was, in that instance, a generous and a kingly
    impulse.

In another while,
Conchúr heard they were on an island off the Moyle,
and his chief warriors, Cú Chulainn and Fergus Mac
   Rí,
would do nothing
but stand by the family of Usnach,
so he bided his time and decided to find out
if she was still worth it after all.
No-one gave a fig about sullied goods back then,
but was she still as beautiful?

The first messenger was Leabharcam
who paid a ceremonial visit
and returned with the news
that she had thickened round the waist
and coarsened about the gills:
all that austerity among warrior-bred men.

Appeased, Conchúr let it be,
but then in dreams it came to him
that perhaps Leabharcam,
a gentle and a loving man,
had lied to him.
So he sent another,
surreptitiously this time.

Tréandorn returned
minus the eye Naoise shot out with a chessman.
With the other, however,
he had seen enough through the window
to bring down Armageddon.

As beautiful as ever, then.
Conchúr knew he had to trap Fergus and his sons,
distract Cú Chulainn,
yet keep his shower of henchmen at the ready,
as he lured the island exiles back to the seat of state.

Fergus was sent, on his king's word of honour,
to escort them
but then forcibly detained,
in his own palace,
by the power of a *geasa*, an honour-spell,
to entertain guests
put up to looking for his hospitality
by the devious king back in Eamhain Mhaca.
Cú Chulainn was away in parts outlandish
on some pretext or other.
It was not for him to interrogate the smallest behest
of his master
any more than it was to shirk
danger in combat,
so the exiles arrived at Eamhain Mhaca
more vulnerable than they knew.

Deirdre, who later on,
would be known as She of the Sorrows,
and not every one of them her own, if truth be told,
came into her birthright then:
she began to have visions of the disaster
that would befall them,
but none, not a single one, paid heed to her.
In spite of years of exile, the warrior dead
and constant flight on her account,
to them, she was only a woman
and with no judgement, like them all.

Conchúr laid almost immediate siege,
more out of thwarted will and lust and greed
for a woman he had not laid eyes upon
since she was an infant unable even to see.

Conall Cearnach rushed to Eamhain Mhaca,
friend of Cú Chulainn but loyal to his king,
to find Fergus' son, Iollann Fionn,
fighting Conchúr's son, Fiachra Fionn,
and ran the former through from behind
before realising what had, in fact,
been going on.

The clan held out,
barricaded in the Red Branch house
and Conchúr resorted to asking the druid,
Cathbhadh, for a spell.
A normal occurrence for the time,
it must be said.

He agreed,
on condition that none of the exiles be hurt,
and threw a moat of water
around the Red Branch house
so that when they emerged once more for battle
they had to swim across,
and lost their weapons in the struggle.
Thus, they were captured
and brought before the king.

Without remorse, without heed to any of his lords,
he had the three brothers, Ainnle and Ardán, Naoise
    the last,
beheaded on the spot.
With which Cathbhadh yelled a curse
so none from the loins of Conchúr Mac Neasa
would ever prosper at Eamhain Mhaca again.

This left Deirdre.
As beautiful in her grief, in her premonitions,
as any conqueror would wish her to be.
But by pure force of hatred,
bad blood, destiny, of grieving,
call it what you will,
she desired herself dead
among these companions of her exile,
and thus it happened.

Not without lamenting the very stones
her chariot had passed upon
on that first flight into Scotland,
not without lamenting the blood of the kid,
like the rose,
on the undriven snow,
not without lamenting the first
and the last embrace
of her lover's now mutilated flesh,
and every other in between,
every warrior dead, every life negated
by her princely needs, her impetuous thighs,
not without lamenting a fate which made her
    beautiful
in a world of men who wanted her
without knowing her worth.

Thus, she chose for herself first,
and would die now,
because she must
and could.

Méabh

They were their province's champions
and each the other's best friend.
All for the vanity of one woman
whose wish to best her husband
led her in pursuit of a better breeding bull
than his, the white-horned animal
which had been too proud
to stand in a female's herd.

All the warriors of Ulster were ill,
kept under by a seven-year curse.
Ferdia wanted nothing to do
with his queen's wrongheaded quest
but was placed under obligation as well,
goaded, teased, his reputation put in doubt -
helpless as the Red Branch strewn on their
　　　sickbeds -
else no stroke of ingenuity could get him out.
There was only Cú Chulainn to defend the North
yet he had slain a hundred or more,
the best and the trickiest that Méabh could send.

Together they had been to Alba.
Cú Chulainn had cleaned his elder's boots,
both drilled by Scáthach, he loved by Uathach
and whelped of a son in spoil out of Aife,
the fiercest combatant their dauntless tutor ever
    knew.

Four days they fought, the first three on land,
the fourth in the ford, cleaving flesh
like babies' heads from off each other's bones,
these who were warriors of the foster-sibling bond.
But Ferdia's horn-skin suit of armour
could not withstand the wriggling of the spear Gá
    Bolg,
unleashing death along the channels of the blood.
And thus the fratricidal deed came finally
to be done.

Alone,
Cú Chulainn would have watched his brother's pyre
beside the ford which held their sundered flesh,
their battle-compact
on the trampled, reed-crushed bed.
Instead,
his man dug out the spear from inside Ferdia's
    breast
and ever northward, champion, charioteer,
they fled.

He would have held the curl of fragrant smoke
tenderly in his arms,
as he had caught the shoulders of his fallen friend
before the carcass hit the water's blood-frothed nap,
cradling the head of this newborn dead
in his weeping,
proto-gangrenous lap.

He would have damned the queen
whose frivolous greed
had brought this dissolution upon them,
loving the soul of this other,
his remains now strewn upon the grass,
absolving him those burial rites
so dearly and unwillingly
withheld.

And Méabh?
This was just another warrior dead
and onwards on her taurine quest she sped.

Scáthach

Setanta,
sent across to Alba,
across the mackerel sea,
deeper heather, lusher bogs,
softer light, the trees,
the sheep, the cattle the same.
Sent to learn from Scáthach,
this bester of a dog,
this boy who hurled his way
across a province,
his *slíotar* landing on the *bos*
of his hurley, loop after loop,
never touching the grass.
What could the adolescent learn
from such as she?

An old woman
who lived on a crag,
the amber stare of a hawk
and the rip of its beak,
accuracy with blade and stone,
the practice of repartee,
the modalities of fighting men
learnt from without
by she who had to dig her own redoubt

and hold it fast, impregnable,
until her fame outflanked
the shame of learning at a woman's knee,
when she was gone at last beyond
breast and buttock and hair,
only a wizened hag
in a leathery lair.

Blood-brothers,
both Scáthach formed:
the wisdom of her eye,
the cunning of her arm,
the comfort of her hips,
kindred by the feats they led
in her domain.
Now Ferdia fallen,
the more conventional,
a gentle and a courteous man,
gifted, but not beyond
the cusp of human power.

It is not written,
but Scáthach may have felt it more
after his death.
Her unrepeatable achievement,
this courtly paragon
of all a weathered woman warrior
might lovingly impart.

Gráinne

An old story. Are they ever young?
And I am an old woman.
It goes hard with me to think I too was ever young.

They wanted to marry me to an old man,
older than my grizzled father.
For the good of the clan,
naturally.

Why? When I was fresh and juicy
and ready for sport.
Why should I conceive perhaps one child,
and that not tenderly done,
to nurse an old man through infirmity
to hoar-cheeked, rancid death?
And then they'd foist upon me yet another one?
I refused all who came 'til Oisín
and accepted his father,
thinking I'd swop son for progenitor
when the time was right.

My silken thighs, my raven hair
and my ingenuity
I put to use and flight.

Rowan berries.
Diarmuid, he was the one.
I put him under a spell
and we fled for sixteen years.
He did not wish to betray his king
or his brothers in arms.
I gave him no choice.
Any of them would have done
but he was the one I could shame
into the long, long run.
He killed everyone that came
and he killed the giant of the rowan tree
so I might have its berries.
They did no special good
but I wanted them all the same.

Eventually, they coaxed us back,
my father and Fionn.
A treaty was signed.
I got lands,
five sons and a daughter.
Fionn was betrothed to my sister.
There was peace.
Until Diarmuid was gored by a boar,
not knowing he was forbidden by spell
to joust a beast with tusks.
Water from the stream
from Fionn's cupped palms
could have saved him.
The old man went three times
and each time let the water dwindle away.
So Diarmuid died.

Then Fionn came for me.
I was alone
and I accepted him.
What would you have done?
Against the derision of the men-at-arms
and my grown-up children's desire -
what matter?
When had I no appetites left,
no, not even a vestige
of menstrual fire.

Niamh of the Golden Hair

I came across the sea one day
from the West,
the land of my father,
the kingdom of Eternal Youth.
I rode a white horse,
her hooves danced on the waves
and my golden hair flowed behind me.

The men of my kingdom bored me.
So I had come east in search of one
who would not.

I asked Fionn for his son.

I did not tell him,
when he left his father and friends,
that he would never see them again,
that in the Land of the Ever Young
there was no time, no ageing.
Oisín, if you knew that
you would not have come.

It took three hundred of his years
but eventually the day did dawn
when he wanted to be gone.
He said, to see his father
and his friends once more.

I gave him the white mare,
I told him not to leap from her back,
the tiniest touch of her flesh
would keep him safe.
(None at all
and he would be sucked
into human frailty and old age.)

I have not seen him since
and the mare came home,
alone.

Fionnuala

Fionnuala was the youngest of four.
Her three brothers: Conn and Aodh and Fiachra,
yielded to her instinct and followed where she led.

They had all been turned into swans
nine hundred years before,
by a stepmother jealous of their father's love.

They weathered storms and changed landscapes
every three centuries, and all the while retained
their human speech and unearthly children's voices.

At the end, Fionnuala led them to the bells of St
    Patrick,
out of the last lake and into baptism, where, once on
    land,
they reverted to their proper human form.

A millennium older: crooked, fragile, staggering old
    men
and one indomitable, princely old woman, they each
    expired,
Fionnuala, having been the first was then the last, in
    Christ.

This happened, we are told, some time after AD 432, and the story is named, in English, for the genitive case
of the name of their father, a Leinster nobleman called Lear.

Iseult

Many are we
who choose the messenger
above the king.
Many are they
who will not betray
the self-same king,
until they do.
Until we give them a philtre
or put them under a shame-spell
or they see their honour better served
by flight than loyalty.

Like many of my kind,
I was betrothed young and fresh
to an old king.
He proved gentle and mild.
This rendered my treachery
that much harder to bear.

Flight does no good.
They find you in the end,
or you grow tired
or he becomes restless
for his old life,
the freedom he had with comrades,

curiosity even for other women.
I knew this from the old tales.

So when they brought him to me,
wounded, I did not cure him a second time.
Instead I sought an end to it.
One love, two lives,
two husbands, two wives,
too much.

Afterwards, I also died.

Dearbhorgill

The cowpats were soft and sweet,
angled on the sloping grass.
Through a gateway,
Charolais and Friesians lowed
and chewed the cud in soft pasture
with buttercups and clover.
The remains of a transitional late twelfth-century
Celtic Christian church,
two elaborate arches, little more,
lined with pebbles,
a memorial now,
called in her native tongue
the hag's temple,
to the woman of sorrows
whose rapture by a chieftain
brought about the destruction
of her race.

After the invasion
she took refuge there as a nun.
In the lore of her idiom
hag and religious,
eunuch of wisdom,
were considered as one.

Máire Rua

My mother was one,
my second husband, Conor, one,
eight of my children some,
but I was the best of the O'Briens.

General Ireton
had Conor killed.
They carried him home to me
all but dead.
Had I not donned my finery,
ascended to my carriage,
and driven the miles to Limerick
protesting my loyalty
to the murdering ironsides,
he would have been the least
of my losses.
A couple of years later,
I married one of them,
and gave him children.
Then I outlived him.

Oh yes, I kept my stake
and lived to a grand old age.
My eldest O'Brien son became
'the wealthiest commoner in Ireland'

and I ended my days,
- some blackguards would claim,
undeservedly -
on his vast and well-bounded
Dromoland estate.

Biddy Early

Am I the only poor woman here?
I suppose I am.
Well, then.
I had four husbands
and they all died of drink.
The house was always full of it.
Payment, you see,
for my services.
People didn't have much else
to give.

The same people
were worth it some of the time
and sometimes not.
'Twas amazing how many methods they could find
of leaving you misunderstood.
And I'm not giving out about the priests here.
Those, at least, I could see coming.

No, if I told a man to rest for a day,
he'd work in the bog,
if I said to make use of a leg,
he'd stick it in the bed.
They'd take the first half of a potion
and not come for the rest –

the vital half – and then they'd be dead.
And it'd be my fault.
'Sure, haven't we always maintained
that that lady's gone in the head?
And what did we think we were doing anyhow
with her oul' witchcraft and her shameless ways?'

Though I never charged them and never damaged
    them,
I never flattered them, 'tis true,
but I never meant them ought but good.
And that is more than can be said
for the cushioned fingers and half-guinea terms
of physicians on shiny brass plates
with College of Surgeons letters, in Latin,
after their names.

The Fairy Tree at Latoon

Well, they all thought the fairy in here
was a leprechaun -
if you don't mind -
the patronising vulgarity.
They think the fairies are little people
who march around in motley daisy-chain crews,
they fit between blades of grass
and hold conventions in the twisted roots
of this totem hawthorn bush -
when we were giants by today's sliderule,
akin to Oisín returning from Tir na nÓg
finding men no taller
that the strap of his boot.

And oh, our silken thighs, our golden hair,
my libelled sisters of ill-repute,
each and all of our love affairs
condemned in the telling,
with a finger-cocking moue of rectitude.

Oh yes. And wherein lies that warrior brood?
- those pampered, fêted heroes -
long since comatose in their marbled lairs?
While we're impugned for every unmanned youth,
we sí-orphans of the plaintive air.

There's an hotel,
as they say in the best of parlance,
at the edge of the wood.
It used to cater to the American dollar
and what once might have been,
and sometimes still is,
misty-eyed gullibility
in Kelly-green crimplene
and mass-produced, varnished shillelaghs.
Those were the days.
Now it's maintained by waiters and cleaners
from beyond the Dneiper and the Don,
while the Celtic paper tiger
has come and gone.

Leaving this shell-shocked, stunted tree
sunken beneath a cantilevered thoroughfare,
spooling out tributary roads
from a carousel
hanging from stilts in the air.

Thus far, I'll allow, well-meaning.

But I can't see how in hell they imagined it could be
of any blasted worth or use to me,
when I could cross this junction in merely half a
    stride,
if I had somewhere left to go,
a people, an autonomy, a way home.

The Lament for Arthur O'Leary

Verses spoken by Eibhlín Dhubh Ní Chonaill
4th - 6th May 1773.

I

(i)
My own true love!
The day I saw you
at the top end of the market house,
my eye paid attention to you,
my heart had love for you,
I fled from my friends with you,
a long way from home with you.

(ii)
And I was not sorry:
you had a parlour whitewashed for me,
rooms painted for me,
an oven reddened for me,
trout prepared for me,
a roast turned on a spit for me,
beef cattle slaughtered for me;
you gave me duck down to sleep in
until milking-time,
or later if I wished.

(iii)
My true companion!
In my mind I remember
that beautiful Spring day,
how well that hat looked on you
with its tight golden band,

the silver-hilted sword -
the lovely strong arm -
the threatening countenance -
to put true fear
in the hearts of treacherous foes -
you ready to go riding,
with a straight lean steed under you.
The English would bow
down to the ground before you,
and not in order to please you
but because they were overcome with fear,
even though it was they who killed you,
my soul's darling.

(iv)
Horseman of the white hands!
How well a brooch looked on you,
firm on cambric,
and a hat with a strap.
After you came back from abroad
they used to clean the street for you,
and not out of love for you
but out of great hatred of you.

(v)
My own firm friend!
And when home to me came
love's Little Conchubhar
and Fear O Laoghaire, the baby,
they asked me quickly
where I had left their father.
I told them in sorrow
that I left him in Cill na Martar.
They can call out for their father,
but he will not be there to answer them.

(vi)
My friend and my darling!
Kin to the Earl of Antrim
and the Barrys of Allchoill,
how well you looked with a sword,
a hat with a band,
narrow foreign shoes,
and a fashionable suit of clothes
tailored for you over there.

(vii)
My own true friend!
I never believed you were dead
until your horse came to me,
her reins hanging to the ground,
and the blood of your heart, from her neck
back to your engraved saddle
where you used to sit and stand.
I gave one leap to the threshold,
the second leap to the gate,
the third leap onto your mare.

(viii)
In sorrow I clapped my hands
and I raced
as fast as I was able
until I found you before me dead
beside a small low furze bush,
with neither Pope nor bishop,
clergyman nor priest
to read the psalm over you,
only an ancient withered old woman
who spread the fold of her cloak over you -
all your blood flowing in streams;

and I did not wait to clean it
but drank it up with my the palms of my hands.

(ix)

My own dear love!
Stand up
and come home with me
so that I can slaughter beef cattle
and invite a generous gathering,
and we will get music playing,
and I will make a bed for you
between white sheets,
under grand brightly-coloured quilts
that will make you sweat
instead of the cold you have suffered.

II

(xi)
My friend and my lamb!
Do not believe what they say,
nor the whisper you heard,
nor the story of those who hate us,
that I went to sleep.
I was not tired:
but your children were too upset
and they wanted me
to put them to bed.

(xii)
Dear friends,
Is there a woman in Ireland
who, from the setting of the sun,
would lie down beside him
and bear him three children,
who would not go mad
after Art Ó Laoghaire
laid out here with me
since yesterday morning?

(xv)

It is my deep and long-stained wound
that I was not there beside you
when the shot was fired,
I could have taken it in my fine side
or in the fold of my shift,
I could have left you to go your way,
horseman of the smooth hands.

III

(xvii)
My friend and my love-treasure!
What an ugly outfit to put on a warrior,
a coffin and a cap
on the horseman of the good heart
who used to fish at the tops of streams
and drink in halls
in the company of white-breasted women.
My thousand madnesses
when I lost the habit of you.

(xviii)
A thrashing and destruction to you
ugly, treacherous Morris!
You took from me the man of my house,
the father of my unborn child:
two of them walking around the house
and the third in my womb
and I suppose he will not be born alive.

(xix)
My friend and my pleasure!
When you went out the gate
you came back again quickly,
you kissed your two children,
and me you kissed on the fingers.
You said, 'Eibhlín, get up

and get about your business
quickly and efficiently.
I am leaving home,
and it is not likely I will ever come back'.
I only mocked his talk,
for he had said this many times before.

(xx)
My friend and my love!
Horseman of the bright sword,
get up now,
put on your suit
of noble clean clothes,
put on your black beaver,
pull on your gloves,
up above is your whip;
there is your mare outside.
Go off along that narrow road east
where the bushes used to shed their thorns before
     you,
where the stream used to narrow before you,
where men and women used to bow down before you,
if they have any manners at all -
and I am afraid they do not have any now.

(xxi)
My love and my comrade!
It is not on those who died of my race,
on the deaths of my three children;
nor Domhnall Mór Ó Conaill,
nor Conall who drowned in the tide,
nor the woman of twenty-six
who went across the water
to make friends with kings -
I am calling on none of these,

but on Art who was knocked off his feet yesterday
at the watermeadow of Carraig an Ime! -
The rider of the dun mare
who is here with me on my own -
without another living person
but the small dark women from the mill,
and to top my thousand misfortunes
with not a tear itself falling from their eyes.

(xxii)
My friend and my calf!
Art Ó Laoghaire,
Son of Conchubhair, Son of Céadach,
Son of Laoiseach Ó Laoghaire,
east from Gaortha
and west from the Caolcnoc,
where berries grow
and golden nuts on branches
and mountains of apples
in their own time.
What wonder should it be to anyone
if Uíbh Laoghaire went on fire
and Béal Atha na Ghaorthaigh
and holy Guagán
after the rider of the smooth hands
who used to wear out the hunt
toiling from Greannach
when the thin hounds would stop?
And rider of the glad eye -
what happened to you last night?
For I thought to myself
that this world would not kill you
when I bought a uniform for you.

IV

(xxix)

My own true love!
And when you used to go
into the toadying, fortified towns,
the merchants' wives
would bow down to the ground to you,
because you made them think
what a grand half of a bed you would make,
or lead horseman,
or father of children.

(xxx)

Jesus Christ knows
there will not be a cap on the crown of my head,
nor an undershirt on my back,
nor a shoe on the soles of my feet,
nor furniture around my house,
nor reins on the dun mare
that I will not spend on the law,
and I will go across the water
and talk to the king,
and if he has no interest in my case
I will come back again
to the black-blooded villain
who took my treasure from me.

V

(xxxi)
My love and my dear one!
If my cry could travel far
to Doire Fhíonáin in the west
and to Ceaplaing of the golden apples,
there are many light, strong horsemen
and women in stainless white kerchiefs
who would be here without delay
weeping over your head,
Art Ó Laoghaire of the fun.

(xxxii)
My heart's affection
to the bright women of the mill
for how well they keened
over the horseman of the dun mare.

(xxxiii)
The scalding of a hard heart on you
Seán Mac Uaithne!
If you wanted a bribe
and I had found out about it,
I would have given you a great portion:
a shaggy steed
on which to fly
through the armies
on the day of your need;

or a grand pasture of cattle,
or ewes in lamb,
or the suit of a nobleman
with spurs and boots -
even though it would be a great pity to me
to see it on you,
because I hear it said
that you are an ugly rascal.

(xxxiv)
Rider of the white hands,
since your might was knocked from you,
rise up and go to Baldwin,
the ugly little blabbermouth,
the flat and spindly-footed man,
and get satisfaction from him
in lieu of your mare,
and use your bright love.
Not his six blooming children!
Nor harm to Máire,
and not out of love for her,
but it was my mother
who gave her a bed in her womb
for three seasons.

(xxxv)
My love and my secret!
Your haystacks are built up,
your yellow cows are being milked;
on my heart there is a homesickness for you
that the whole province of Munster will not cure
nor the smiths of Oileán na bhFionn.
Until Art Ó Laoghaire returns to me,
the loneliness will not go away
that is pressing on my heart's core,

shut up tight
like a trunk that is locked up
and the key gone astray.

(xxxvi)
Women out there weeping
stay on your feet
until Art Mhac Conchubhair calls for a drink,
and extra for the poor,
before he goes into that school -
not to study learning or music
but to carry clay and stones.

Rough Pronunciation Guide

For those who would like to know how to pronounce the (unpronounceable to the uninitiated) Gaelic words and names used in the poems, bearing in mind that pronounciation of any Gaelic words varies according to region and dialect. These are (mostly) my (Munster dialect) approximations (for native speakers of English).

Aife	Eefah
Ainle	Awinleh
Alba (Scotland)	Awlba
Allchoill	Awlcwill
Aodh	A (as in 'say')
Ardán	Ardawn
Art Ó Laoghaire	Art O'Leary
Béal Atha na Ghaorthaigh	Bale Awha na Gwayrhig
Bós	boss
Caolcnoc	Cwaolcnuck
Carraig an Íme	Cawrig an Eemeh
Cathbhad	Cahwad
Céadach	Cayduck
Ceaplaing	Kyapling

Cill na Martar	Kill nah Mawrtahr
Conall	Cohnal
Conall Cearnach	Cohnal Kyarnock
Conchúr Mac Neasa	Crohoor Mac Nyasa (Connor)
Conn	Con
Croí	cree
Cú Chulainn	Cucullen
Dearbhorgill	Dervorgill
Diarmuid	Deermwid
Doire Fhíonáin	Dihreh Fyonnawn (Derryfinnane)
Domhnaill Mór Ó Chonaill	Dohnal Mowr Oh Conayl
Eamhain Mhaca	Awin Wawka
Eibhlín Dhubh Ní Chonaill	Eileen Duv Nee Conayl
Fear O Laoghaire	Farr O Leary
Ferdia	Ferdya
Fergus Mac Rí	Fergus Mac Ree
Fiachra Fionn	Fyakra Fyon
Fionnuala	Fyonooala
Gá Bolg	Gaw Bollug
Gaortha	Gwayrha
Geasa (honour spell)	Gyasa
Gráinne	Grania
Greannach	Grannuck
Guagán	Googawn

Iollann Fionn	Yollan Fyon
Laoiseach	Leeshuck
Leabharcam	Lauwarcam
Lear	Lahr
Máire Rua	Mawyreh Ruah
Méabh	Maeve
Naoise	Neesha
Niamh	Neeav
Oileán na bhFionn	Ihlawn nah Vyon
Oisín	Usheen
Scáthach	Scahok
Seán Mac Uaithne	Shawn Mack Oohneh
Setanta	Saytanta
Slíotar	Shlither
Tír na n-Óg	Teer na Nogue
Tréandorn	Traindorn
Uathach	Oothack
Uíbh Laoghaire	Eave Leary
Usnach	Ushnock
Uisnigh	Ishnick

www.ingramcontent.com/pod-product-compliance
Lightning Source LLC
Chambersburg PA
CBHW061249040426
42444CB00010B/2314